PRETTY LITTLE THINGS COLORING BOOK

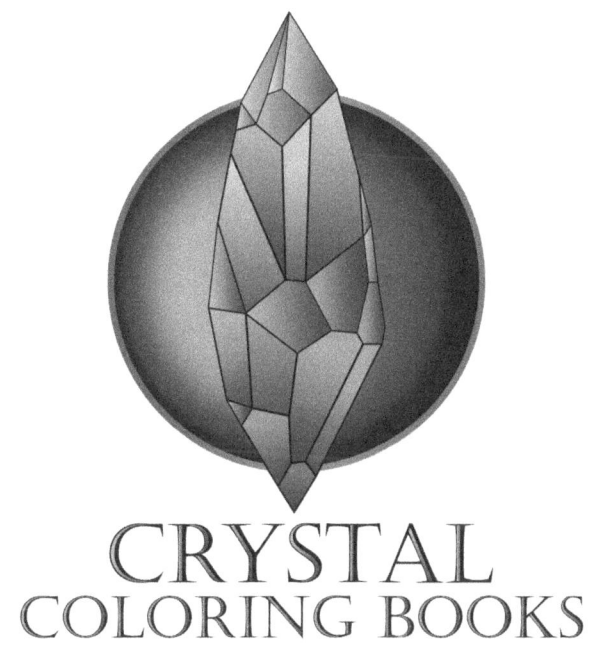

Copyright © 2018 Crystal Coloring Books
All rights reserved.

ISBN: 9781797936277

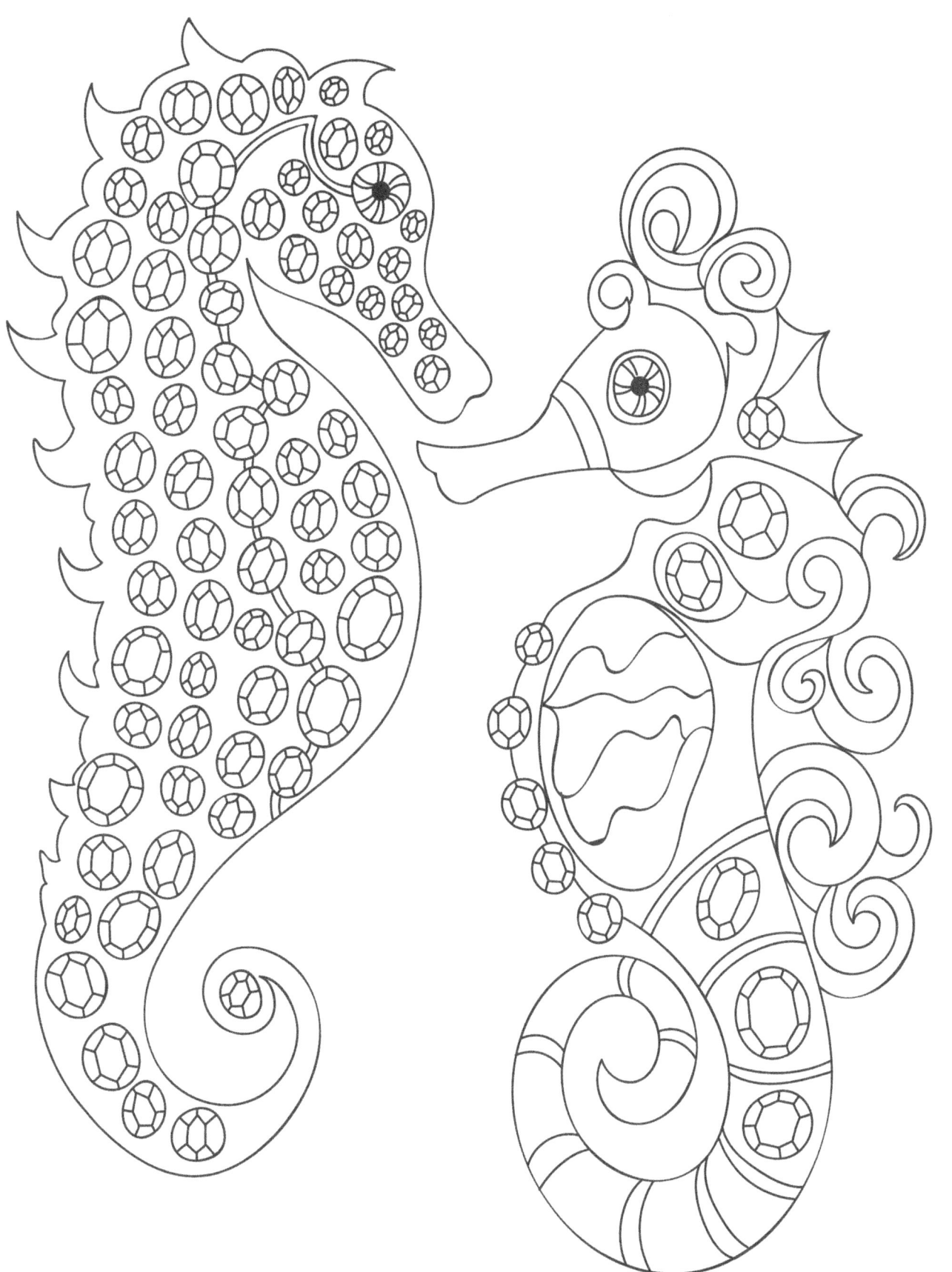

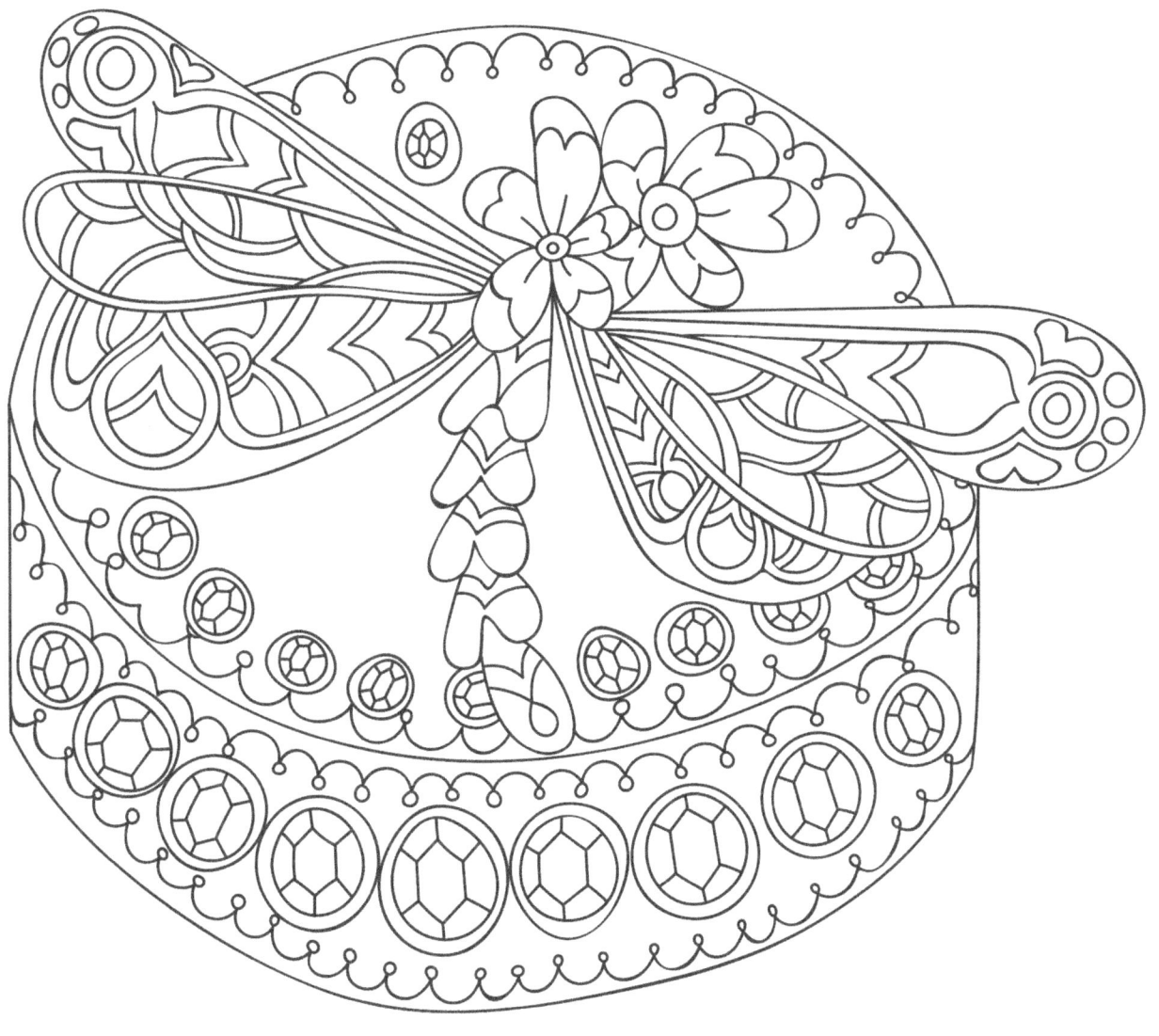

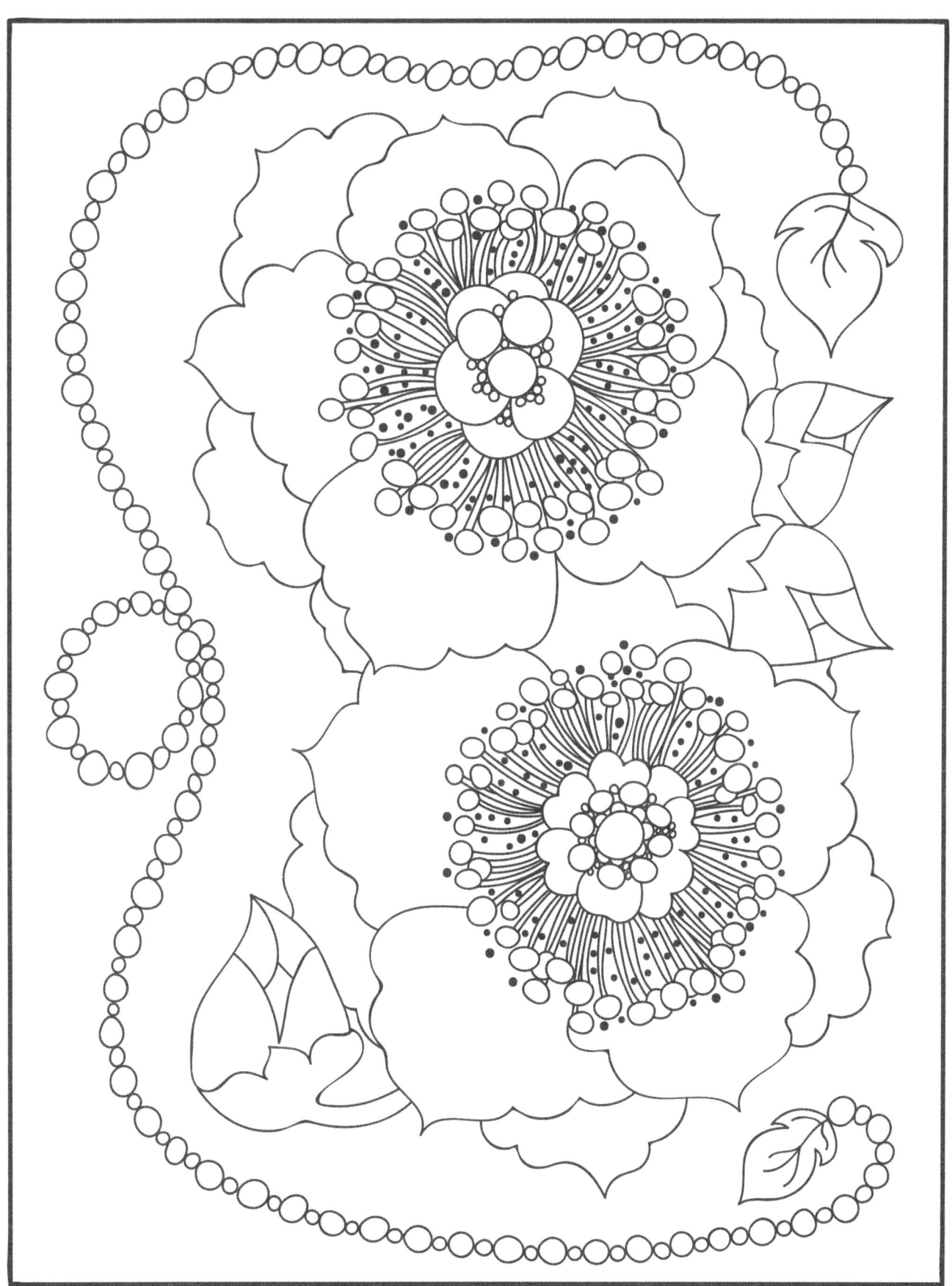

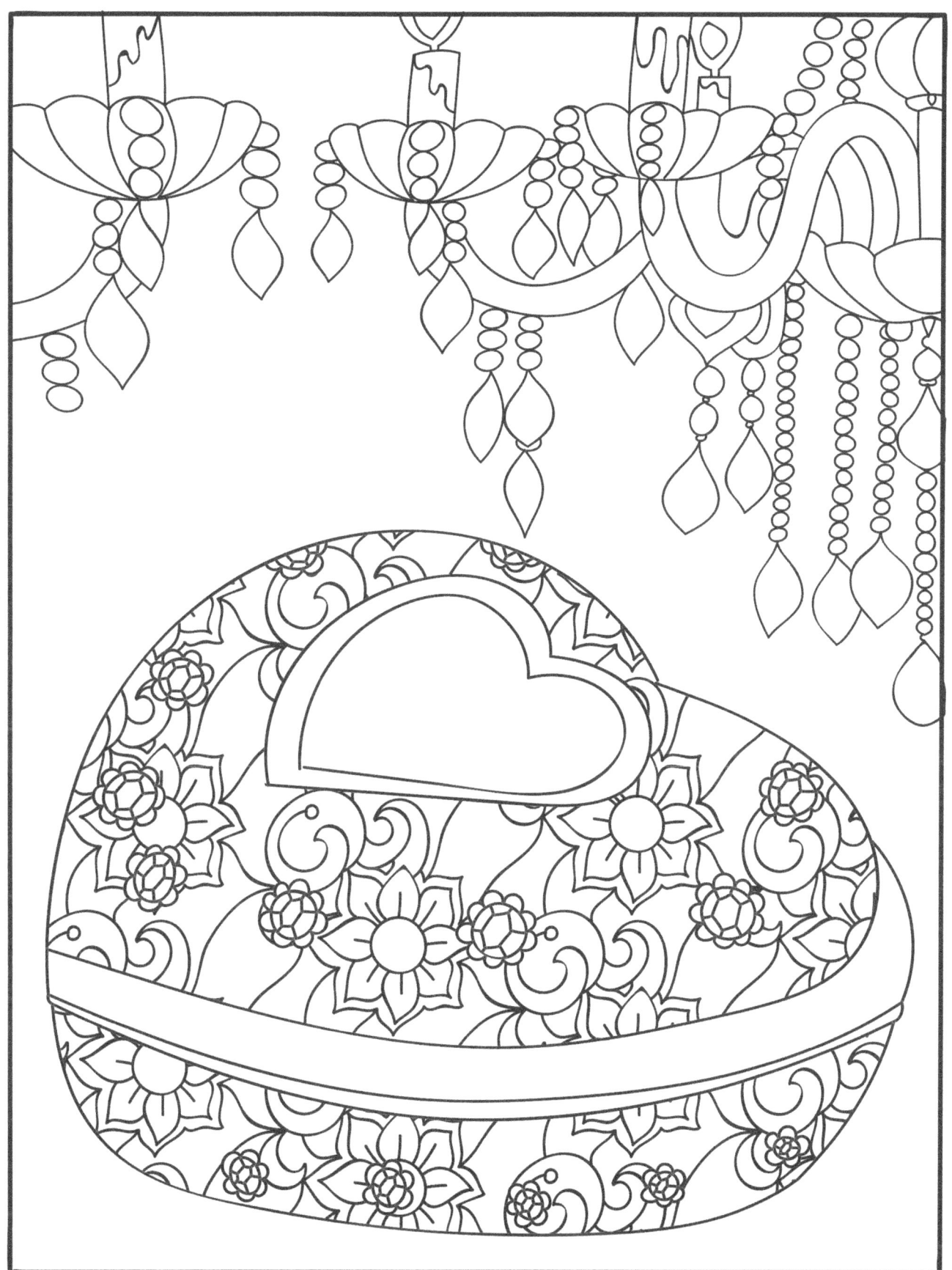

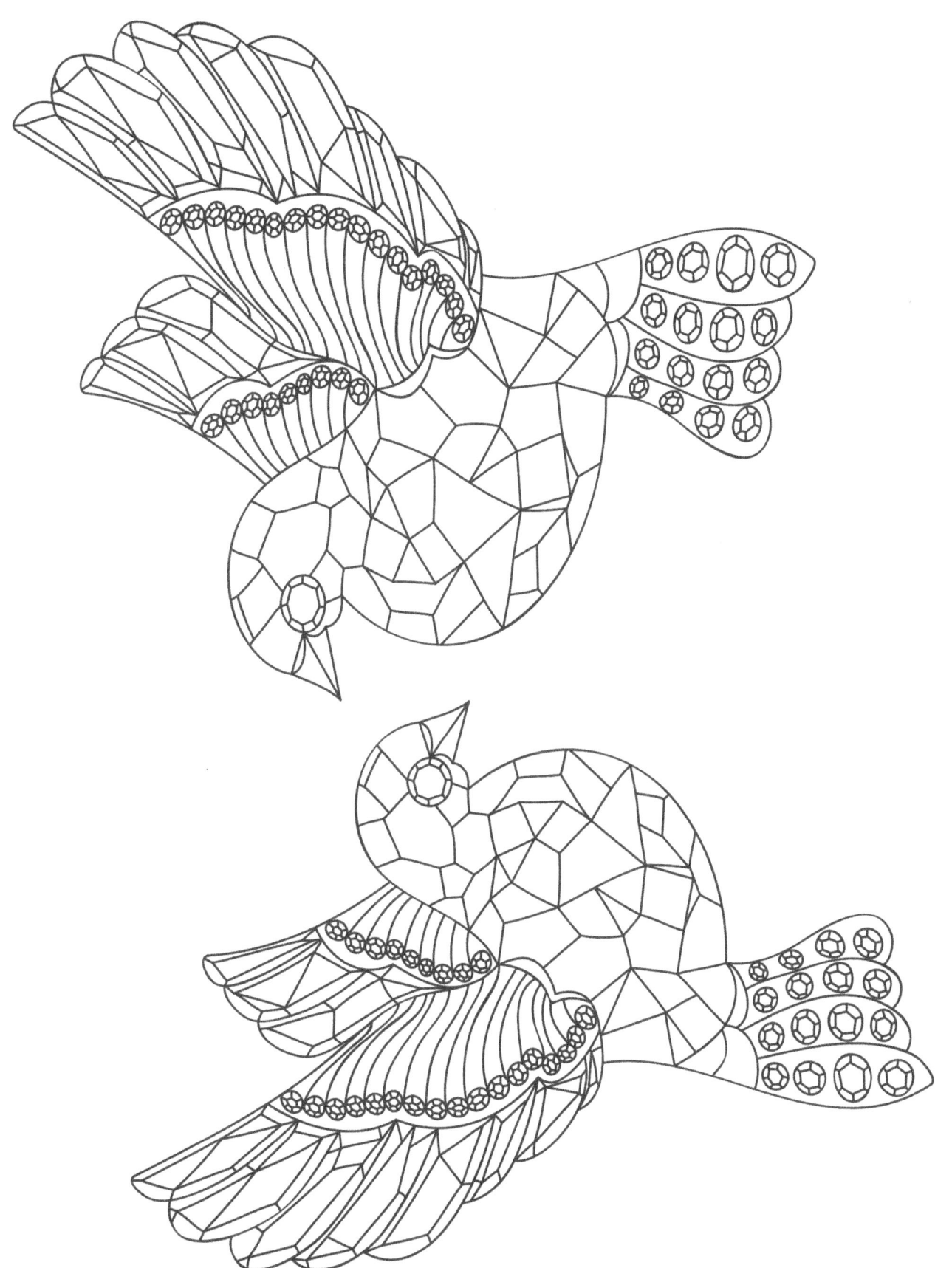

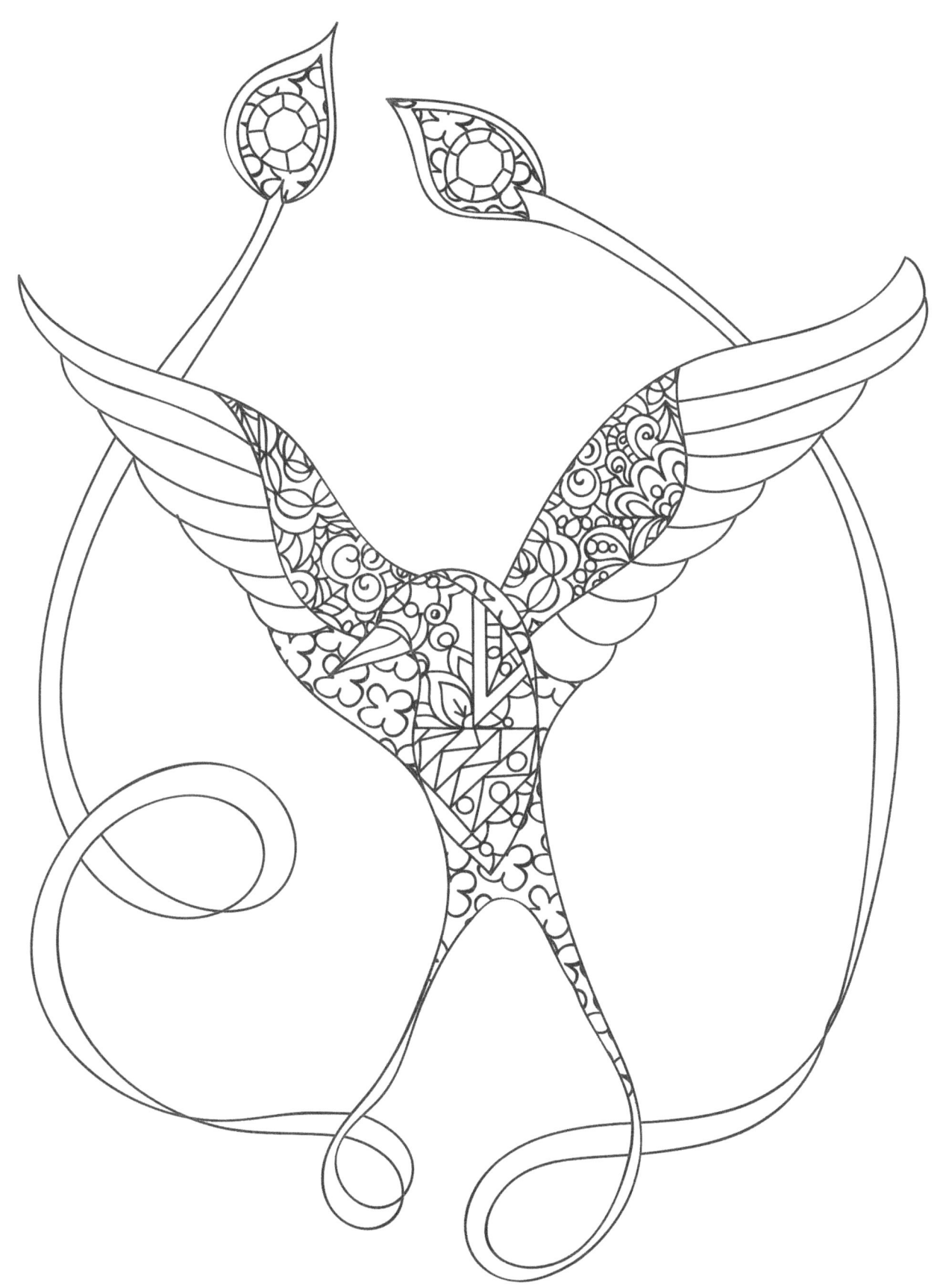

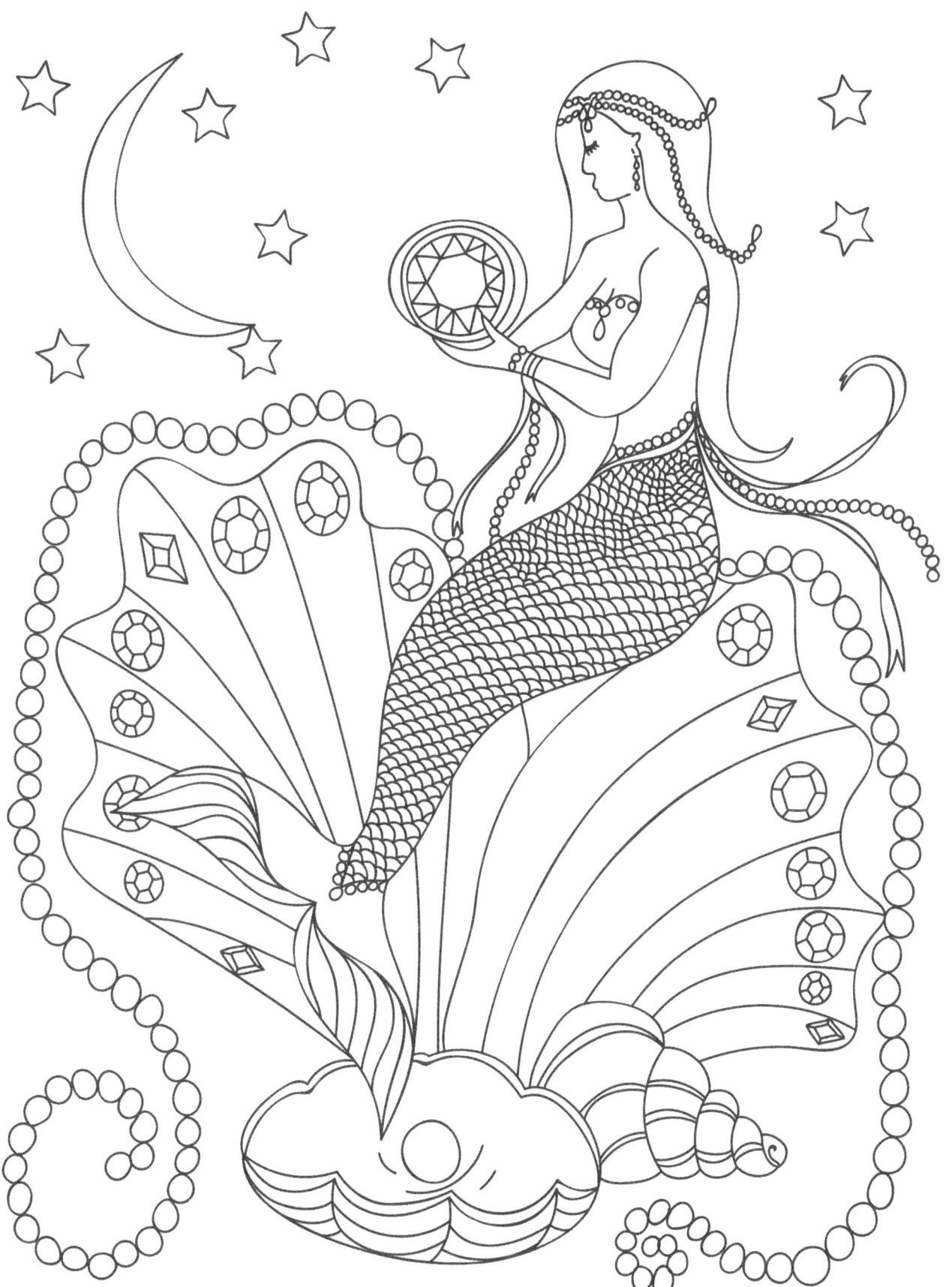

PRETTY LITTLE THINGS

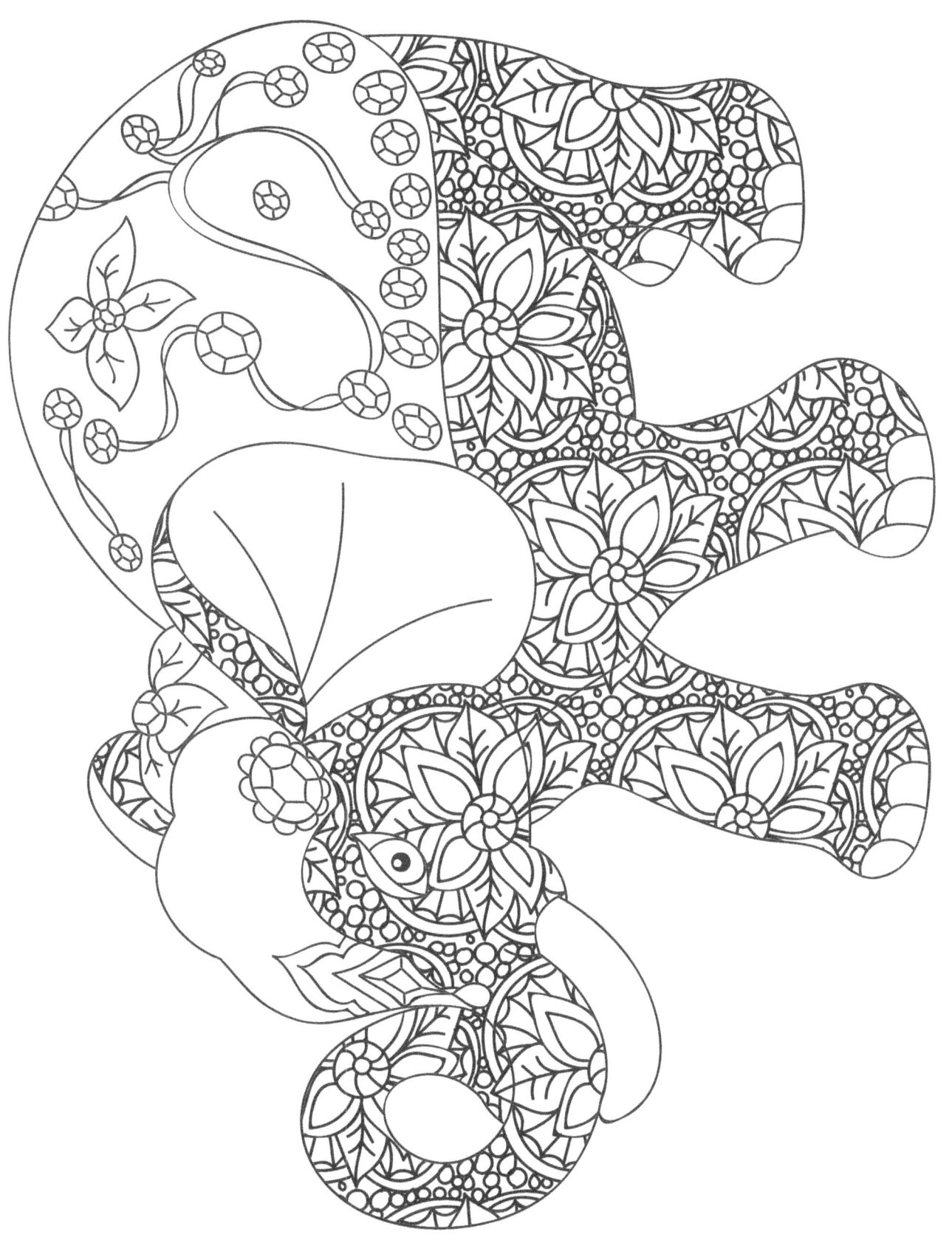

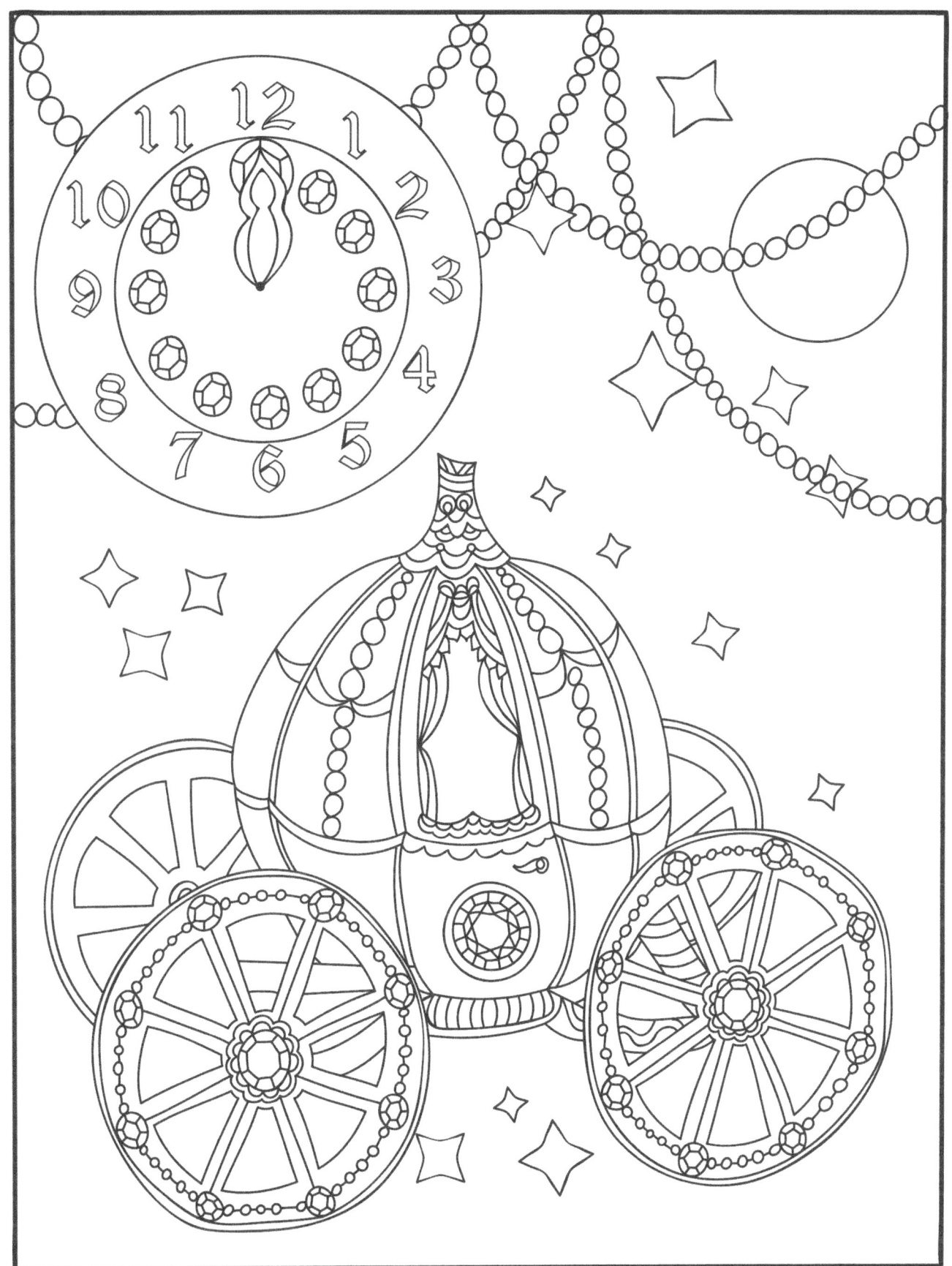

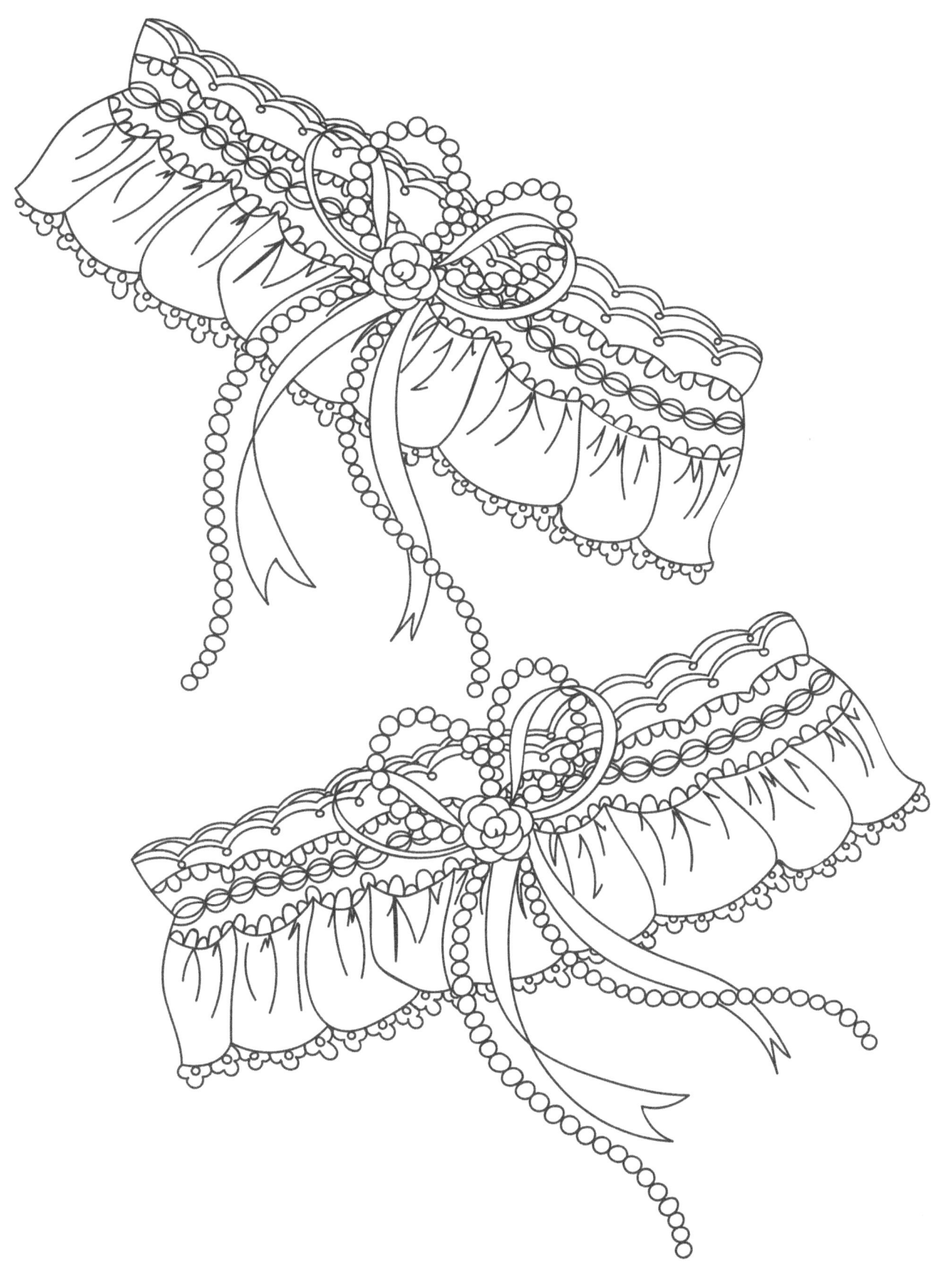

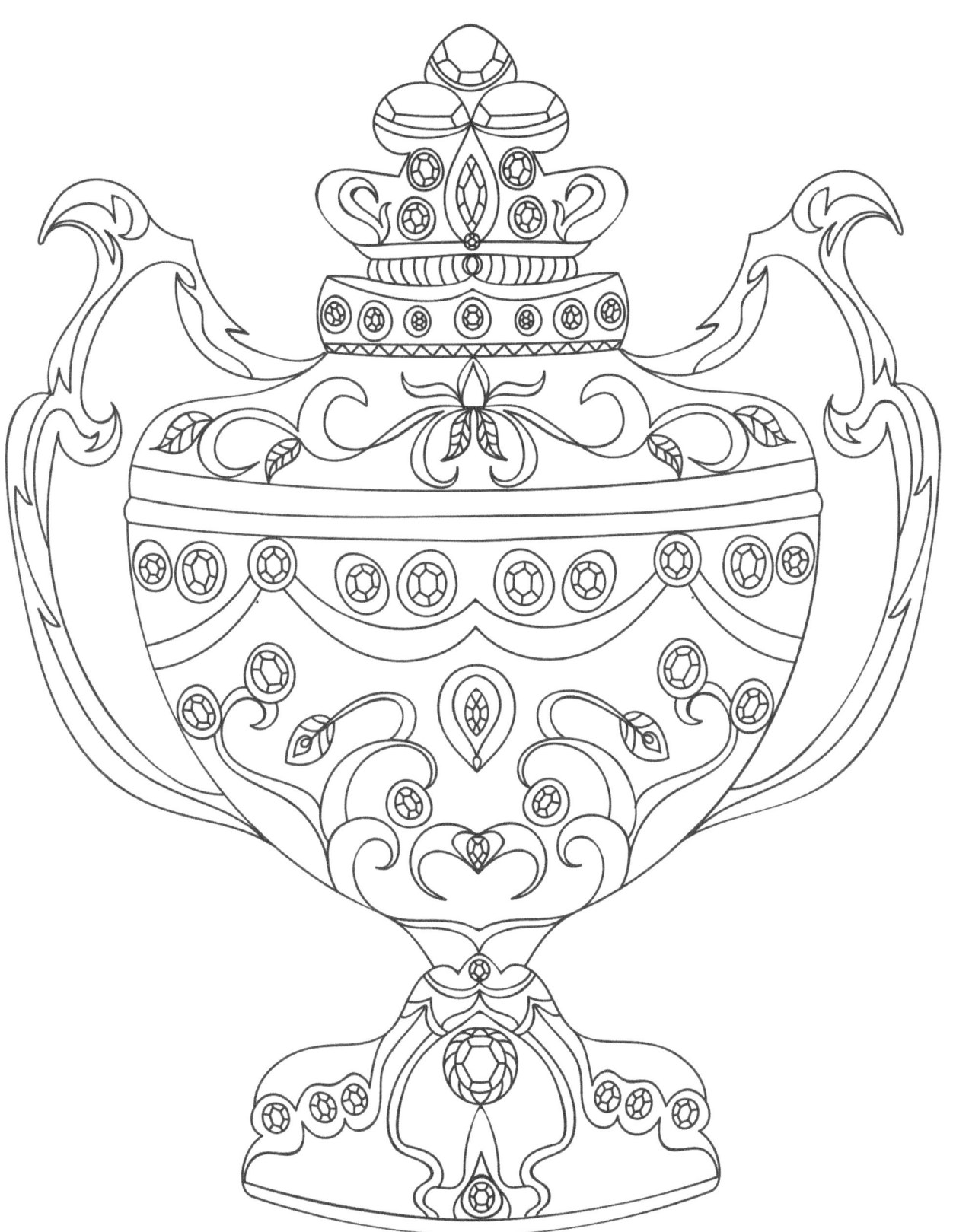

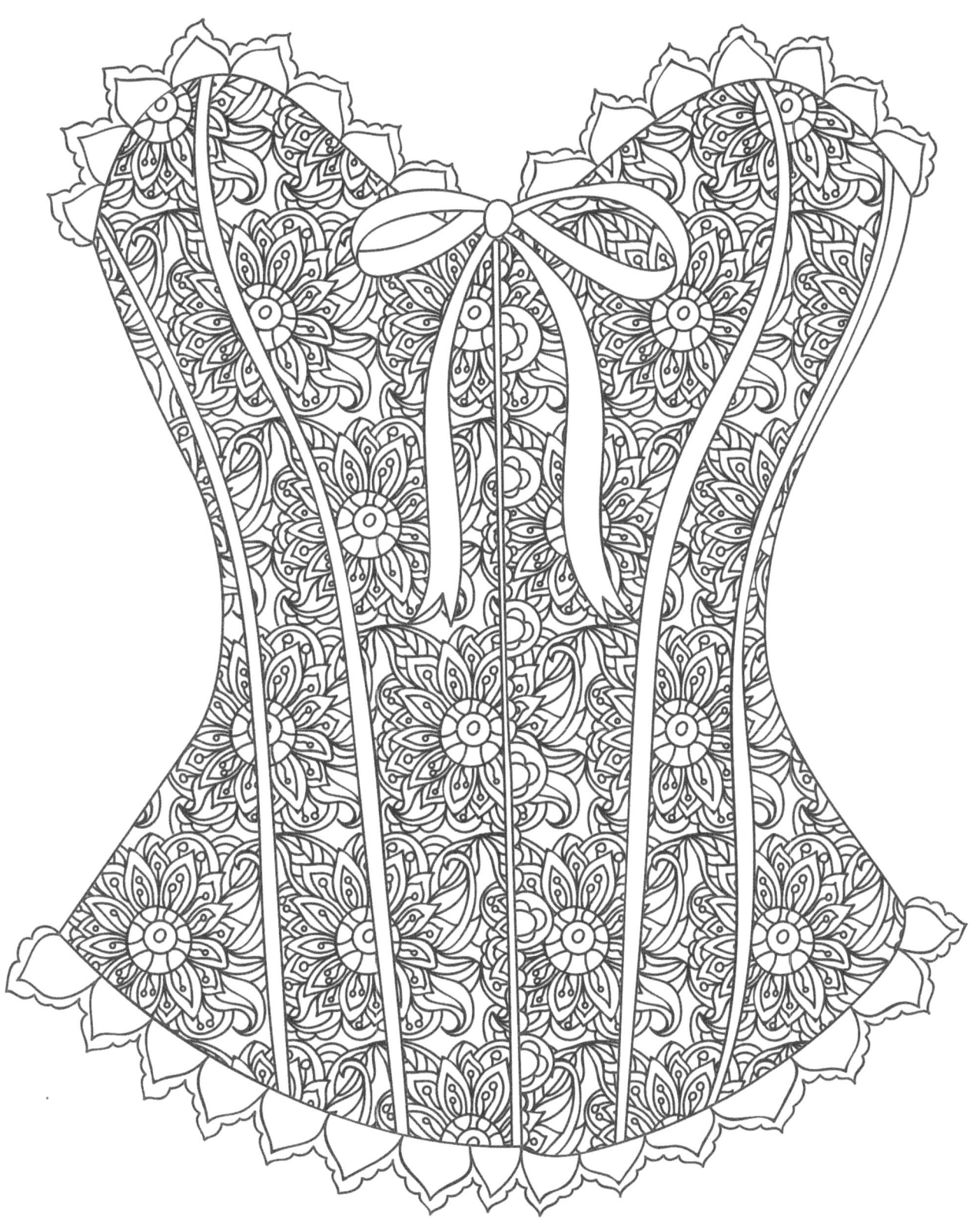

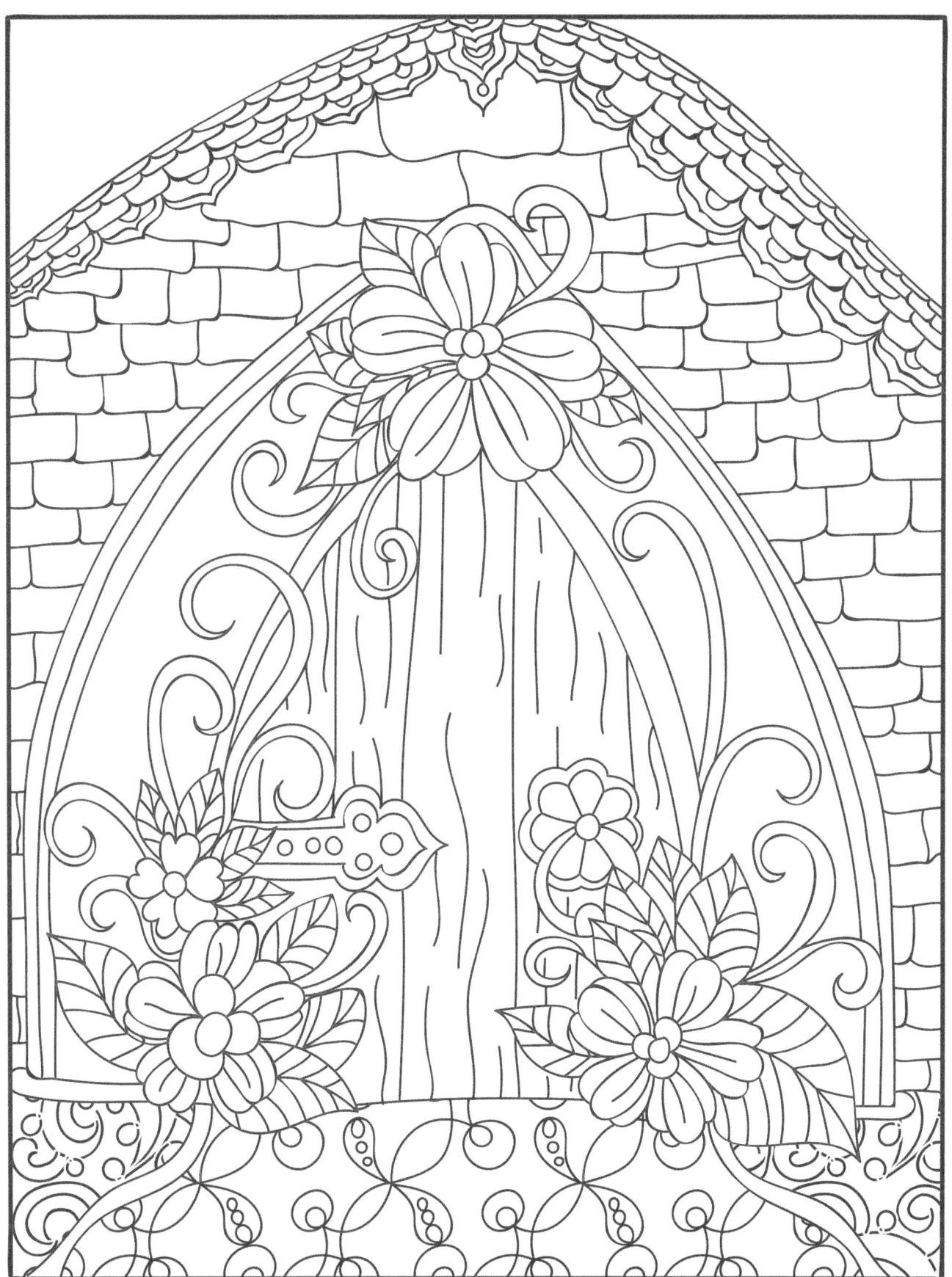

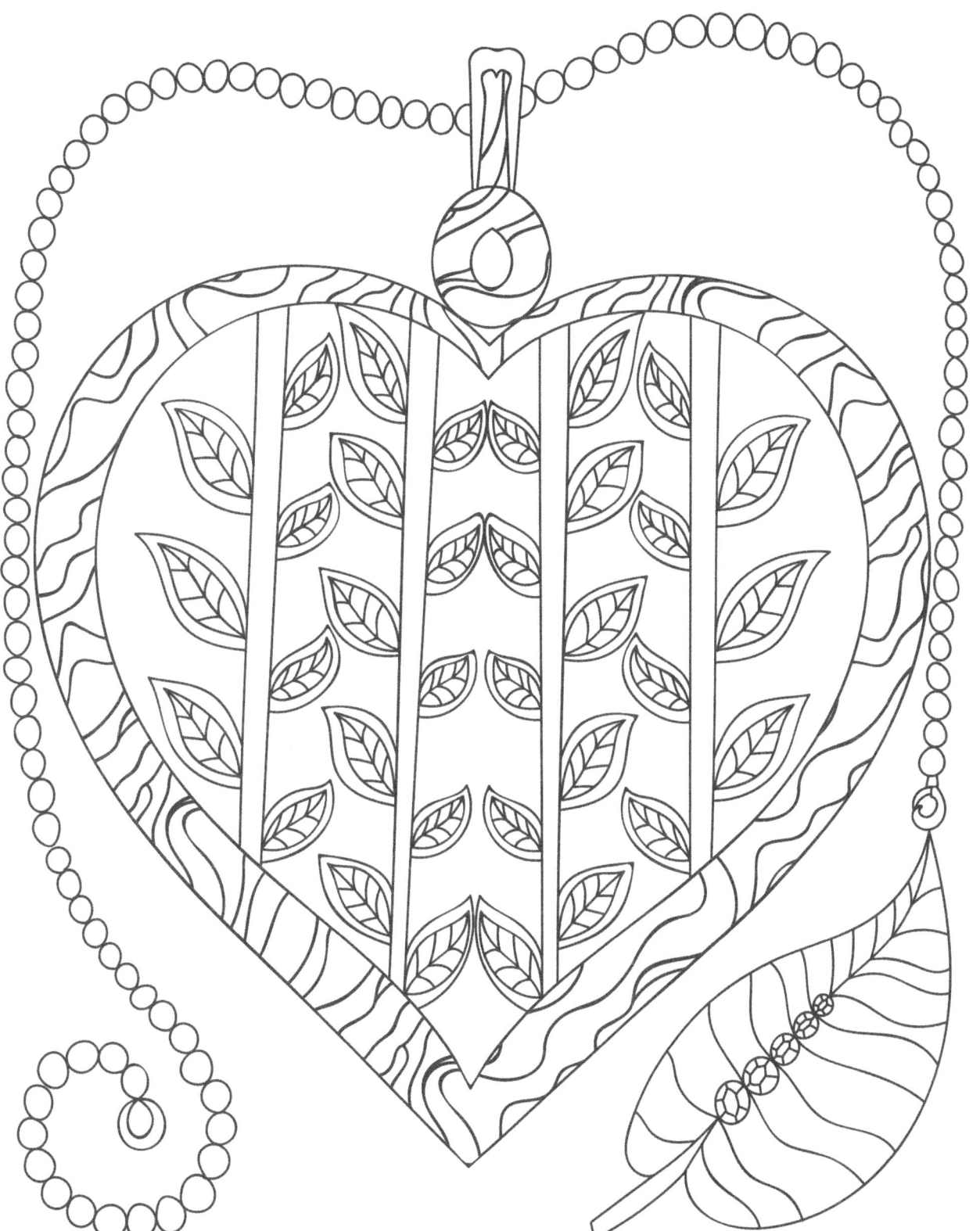

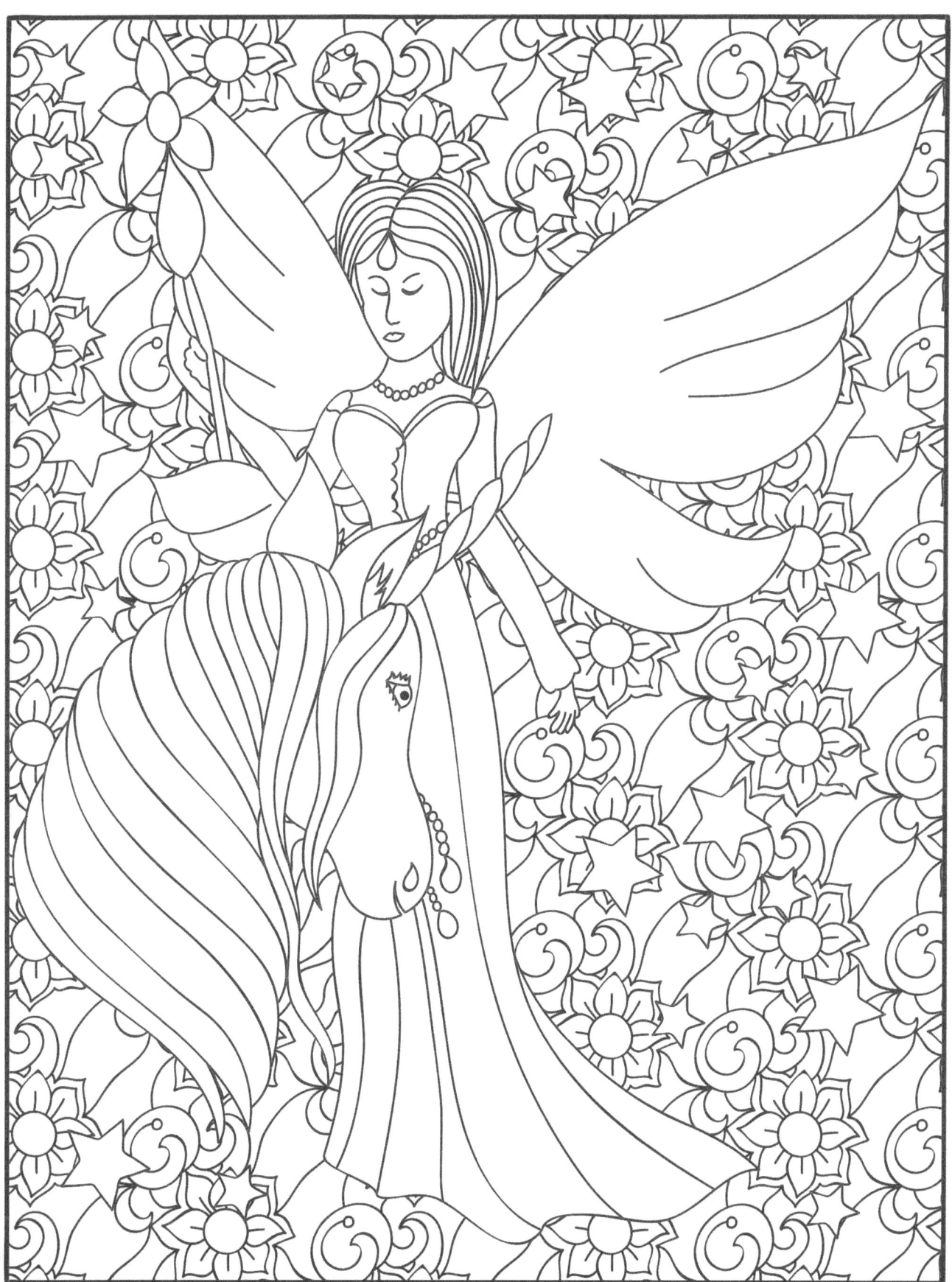

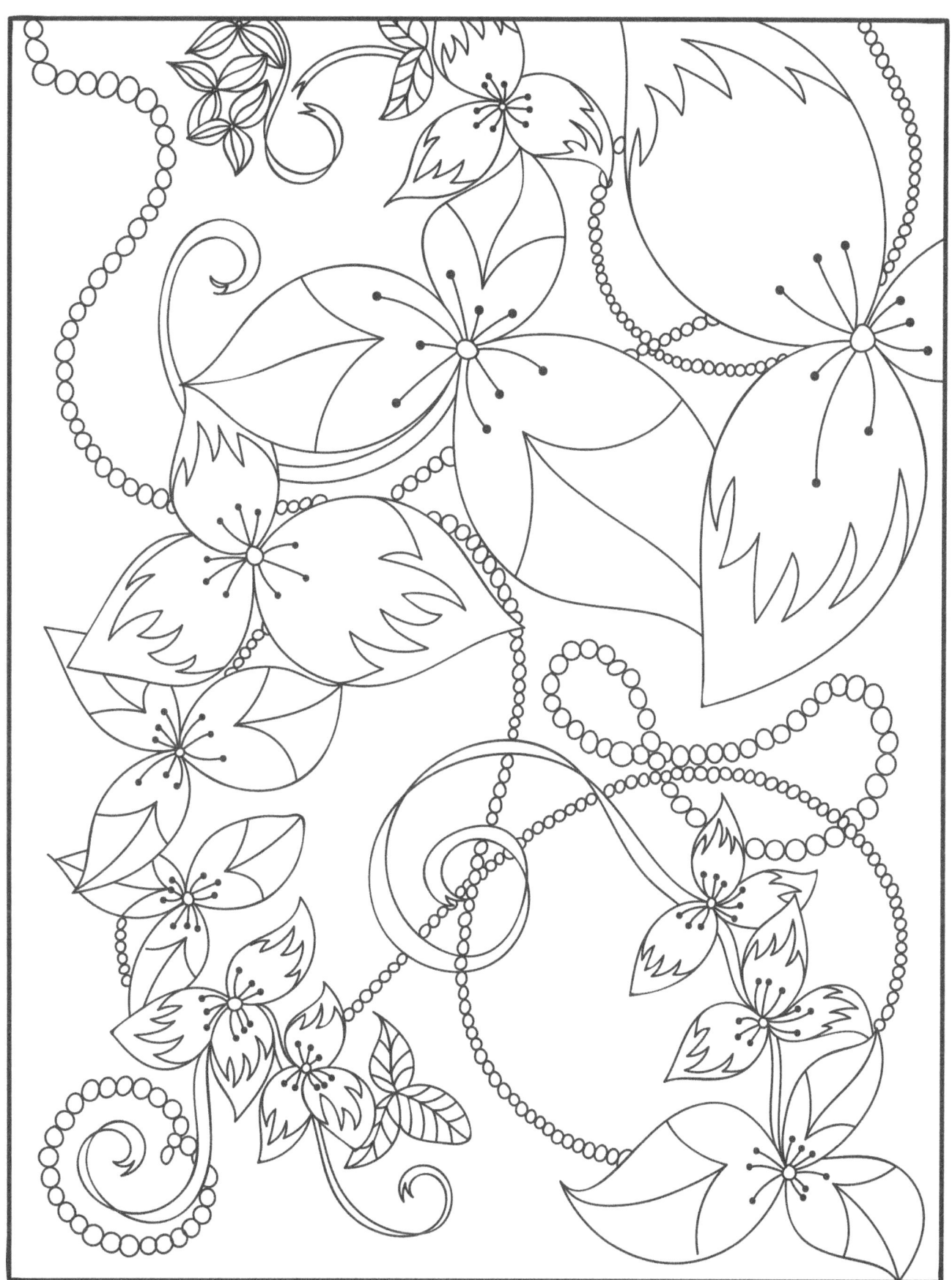

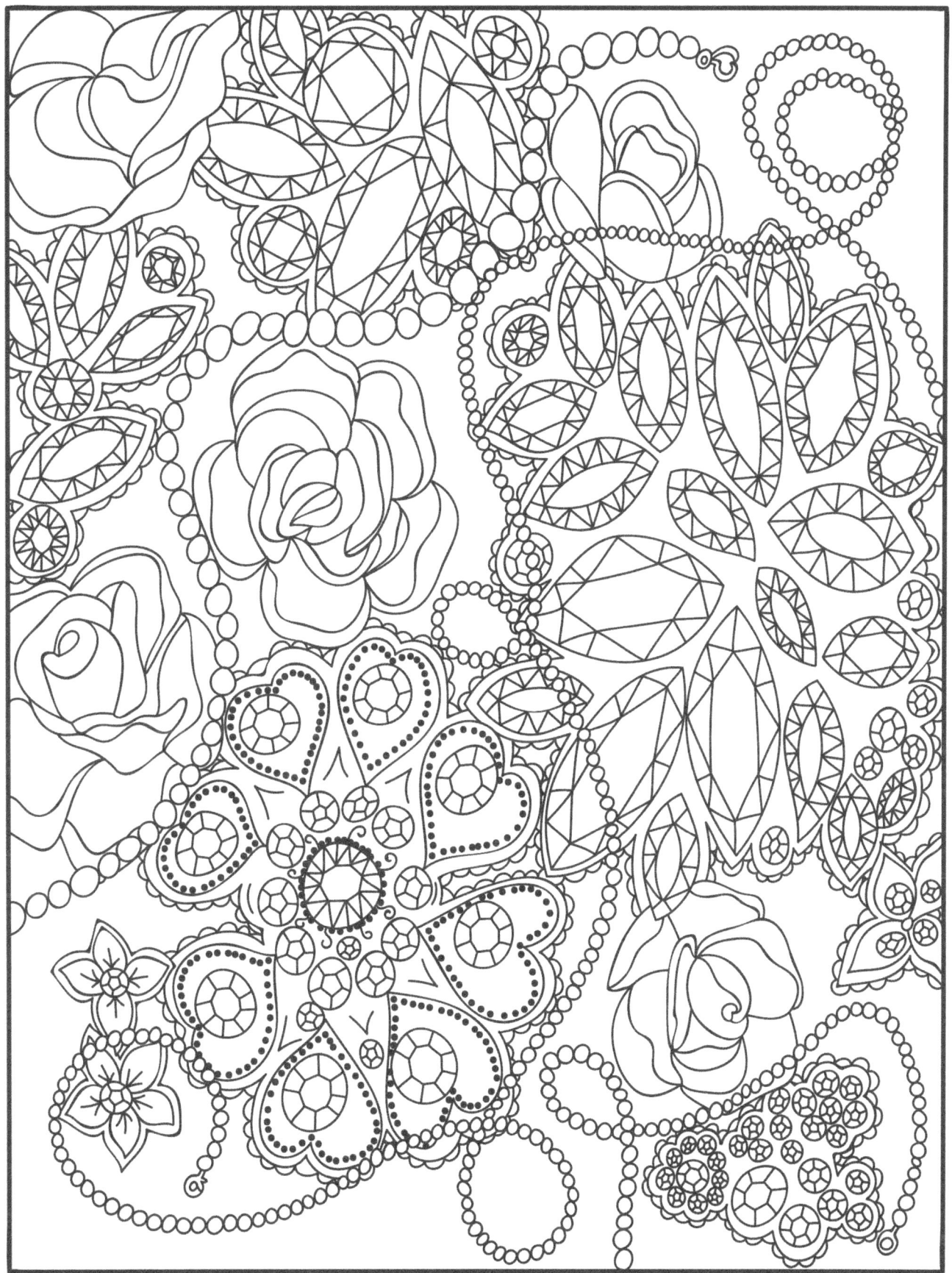

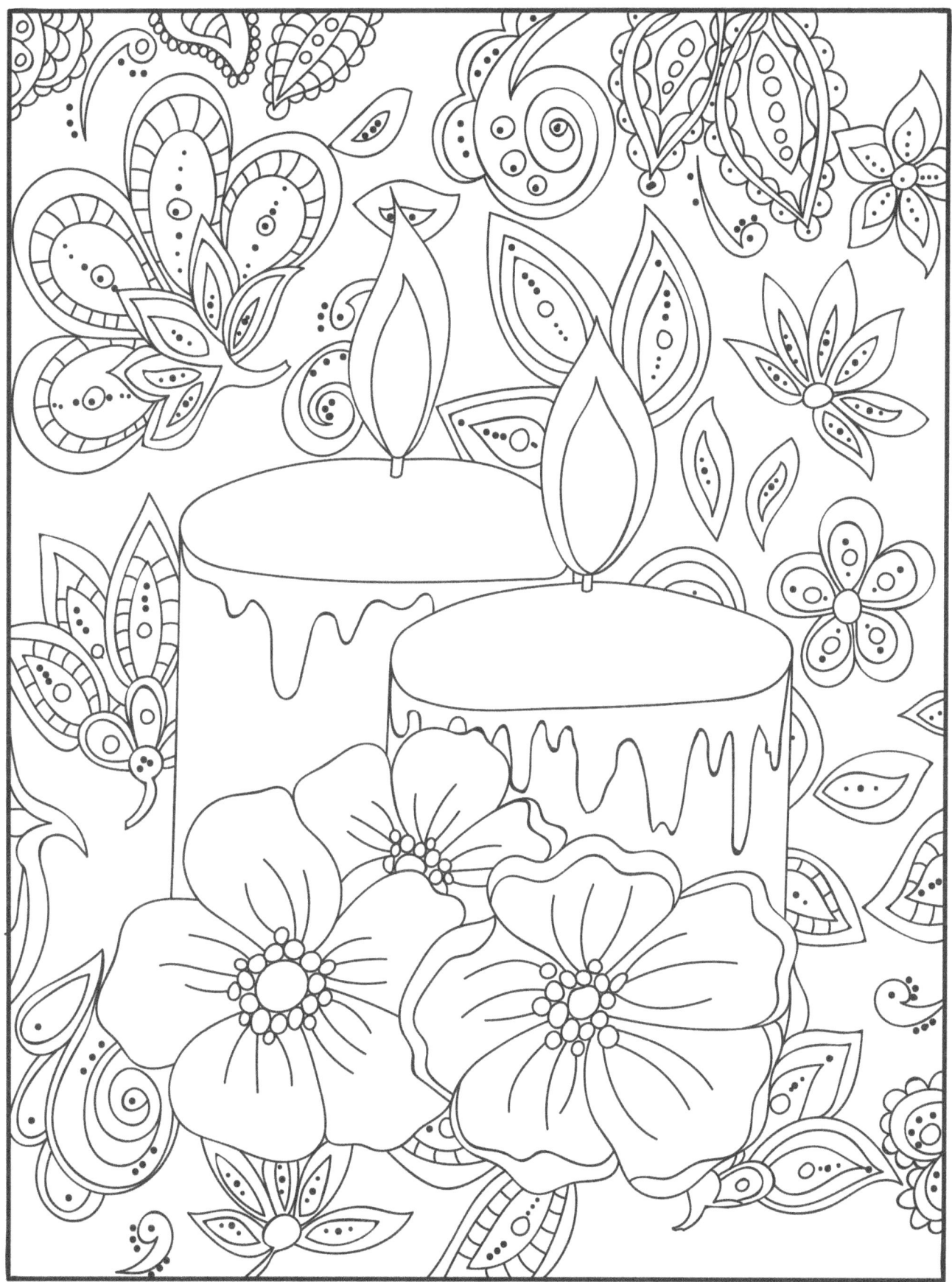

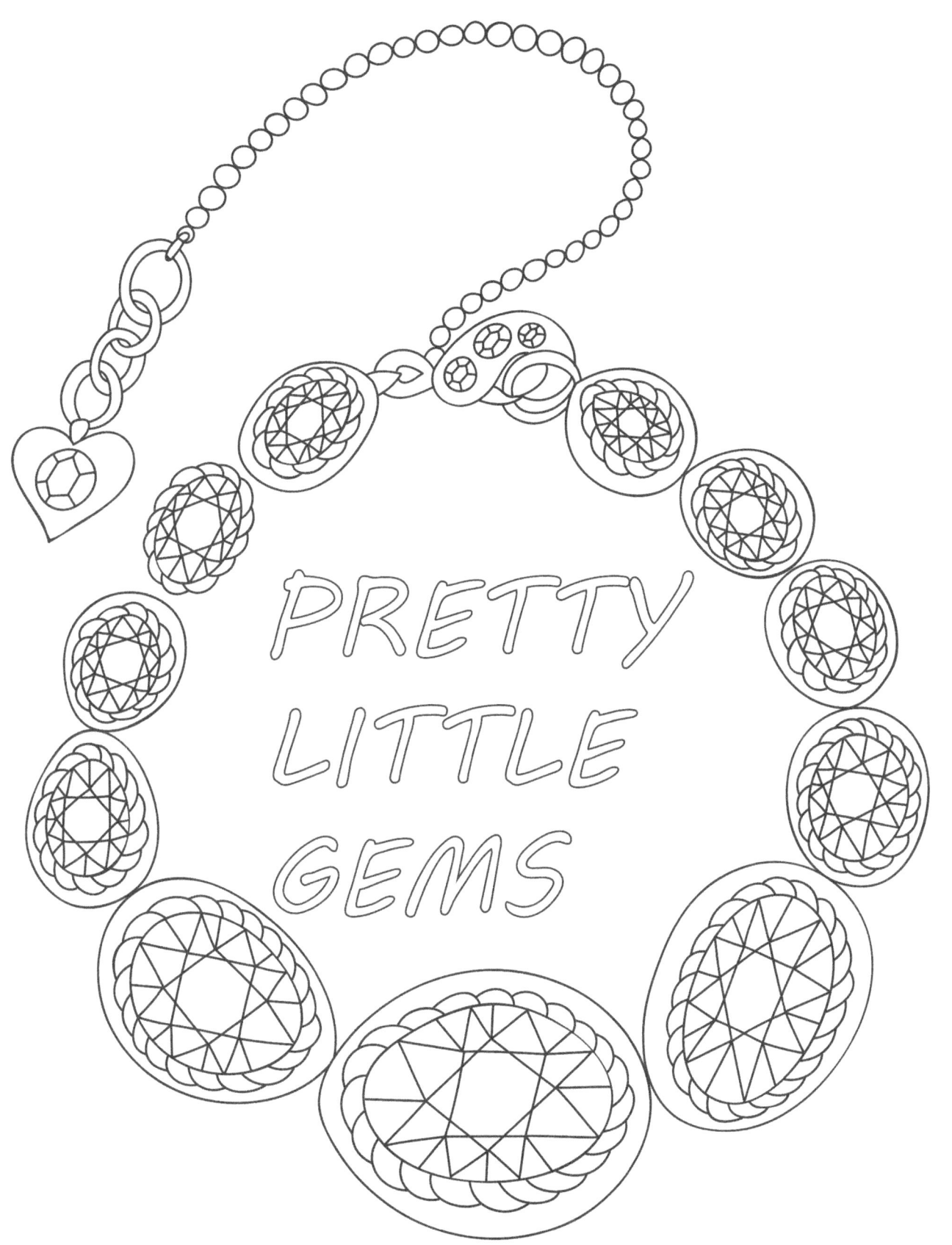

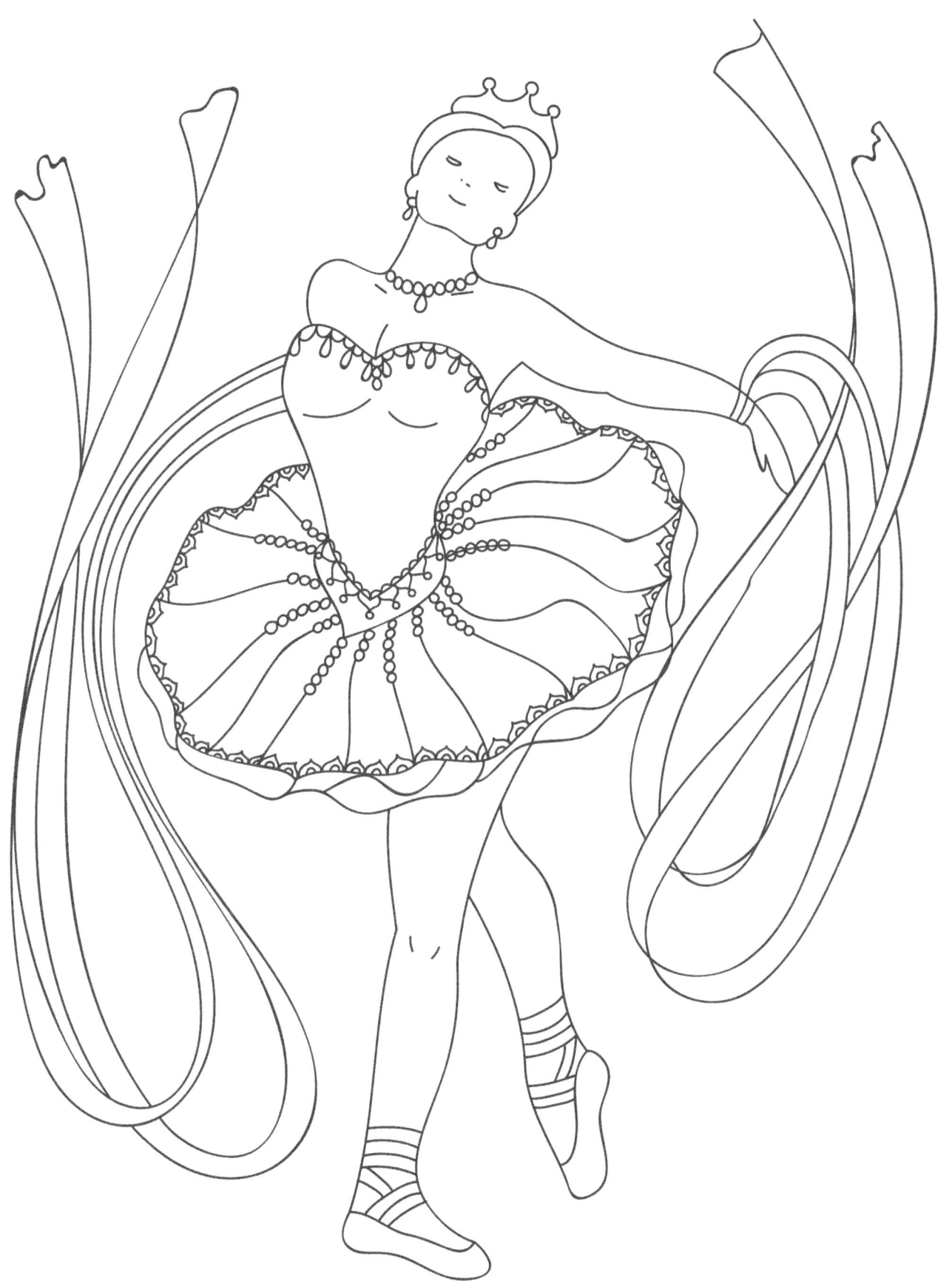

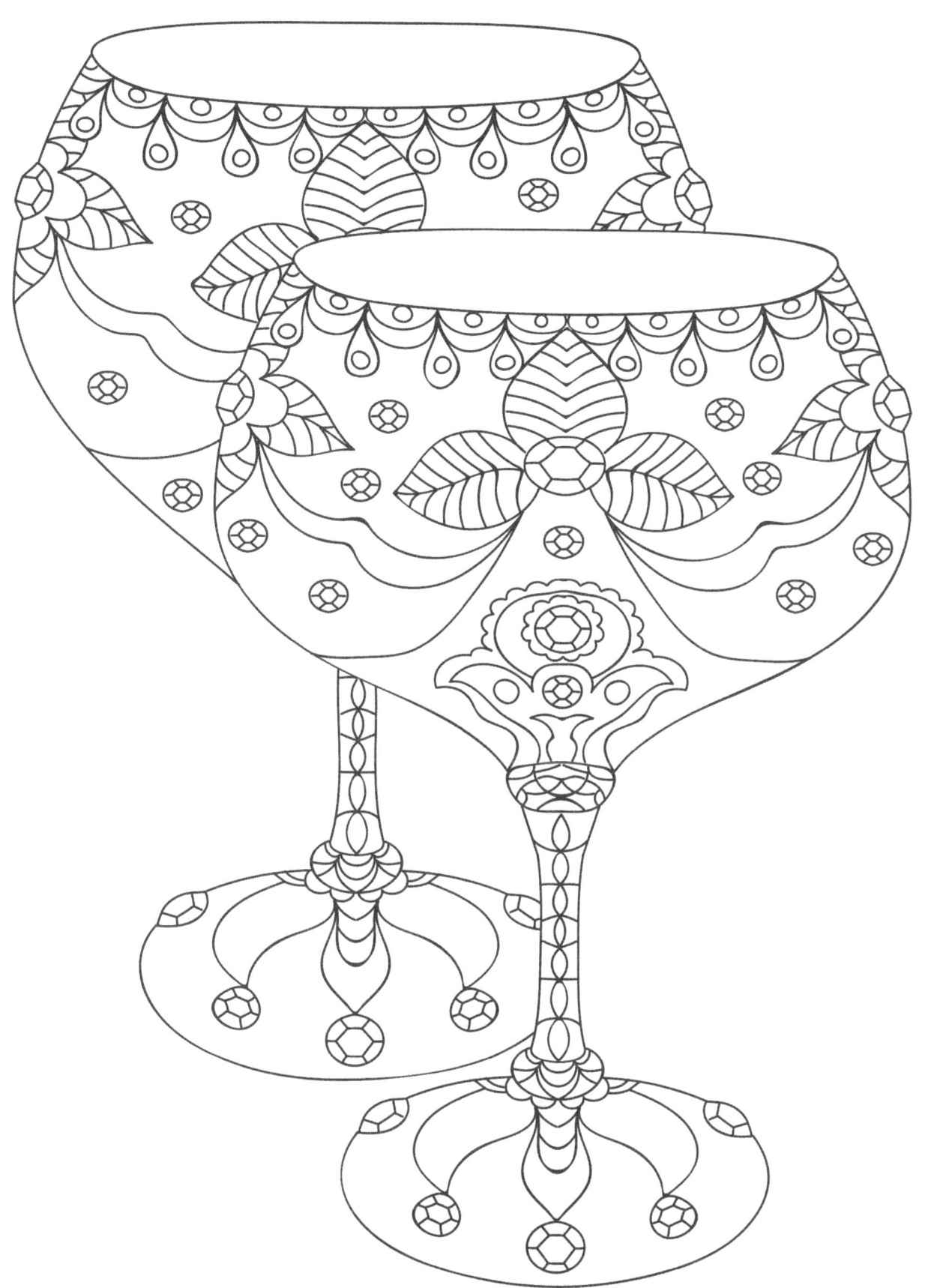

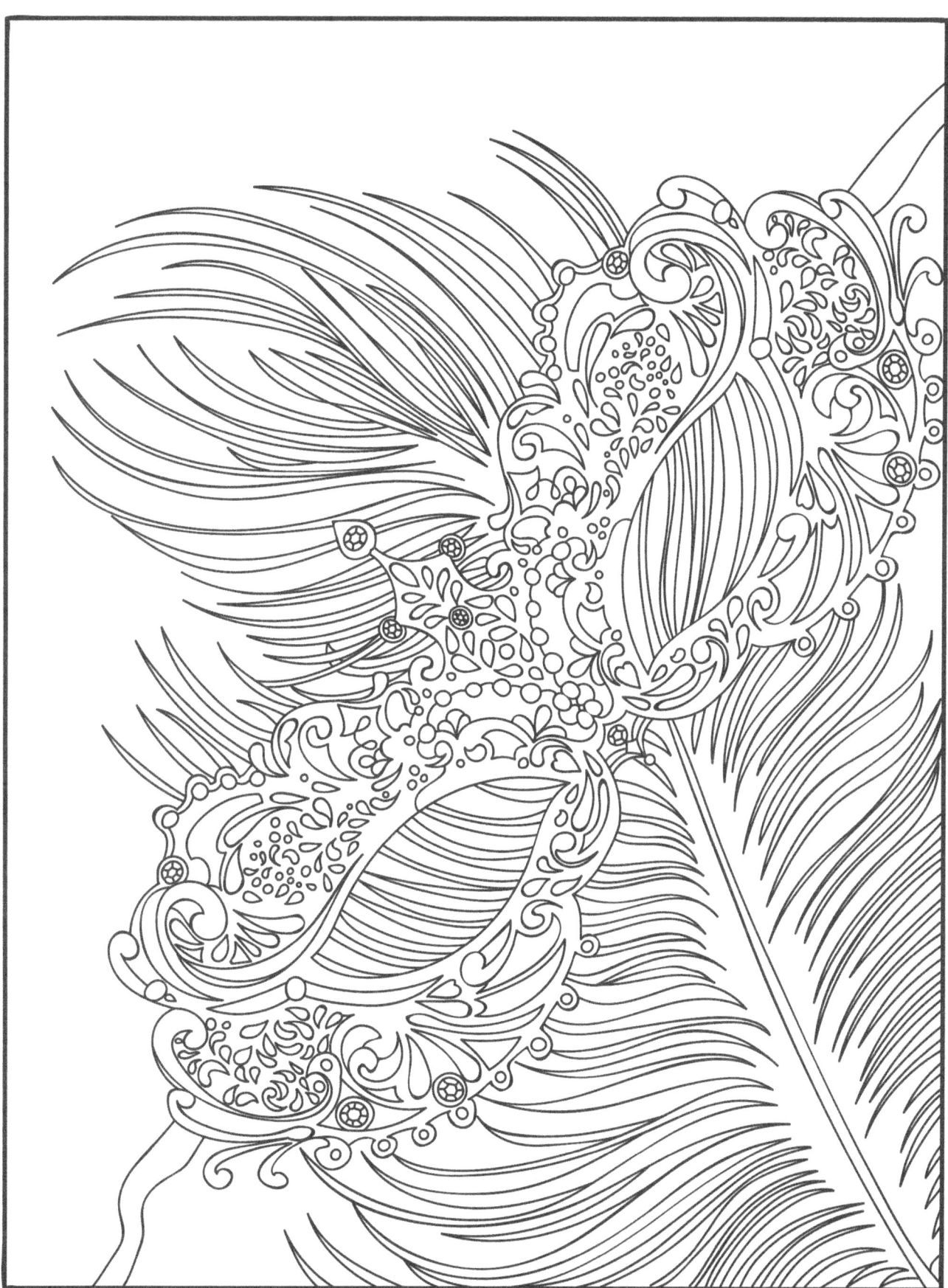

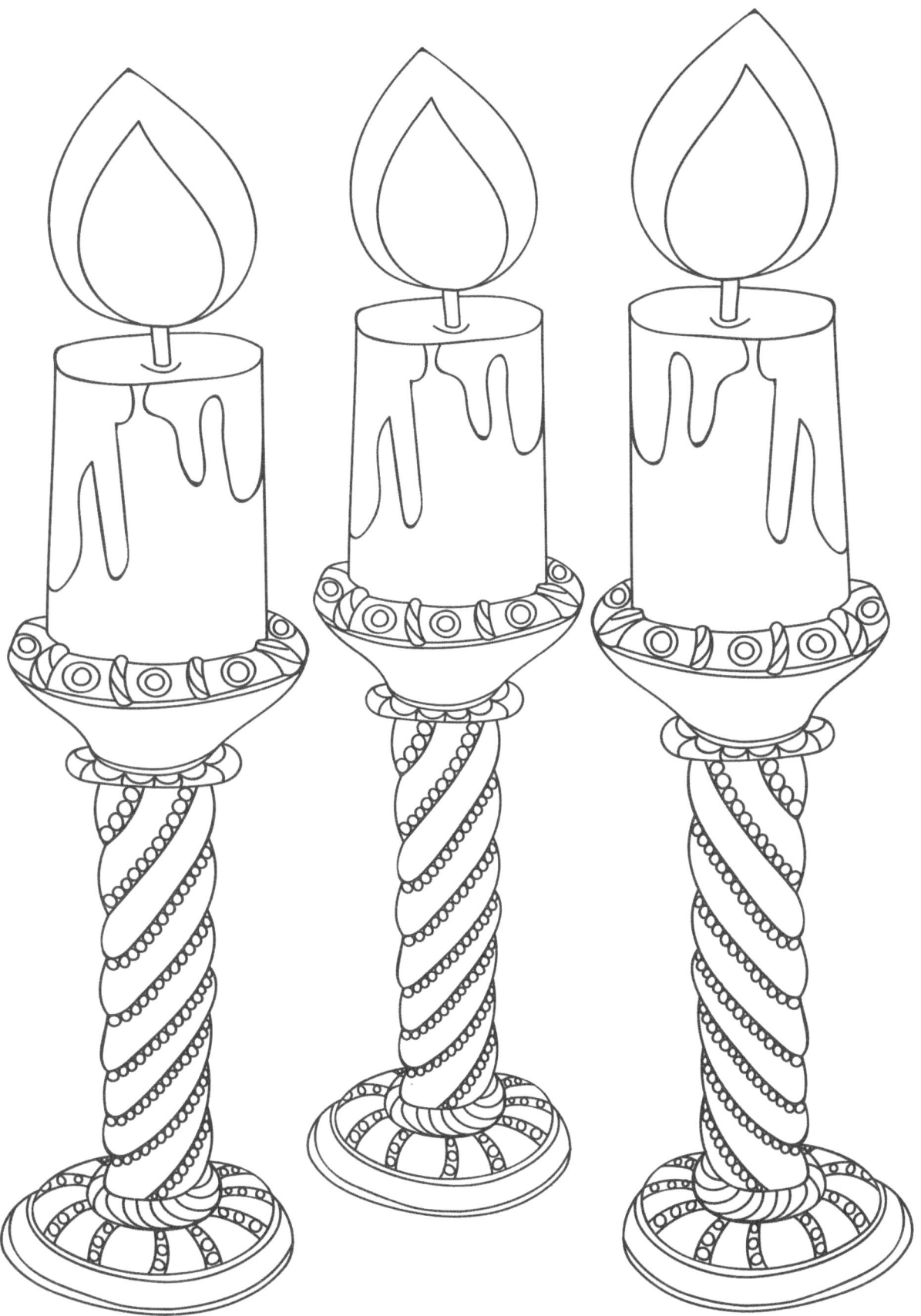

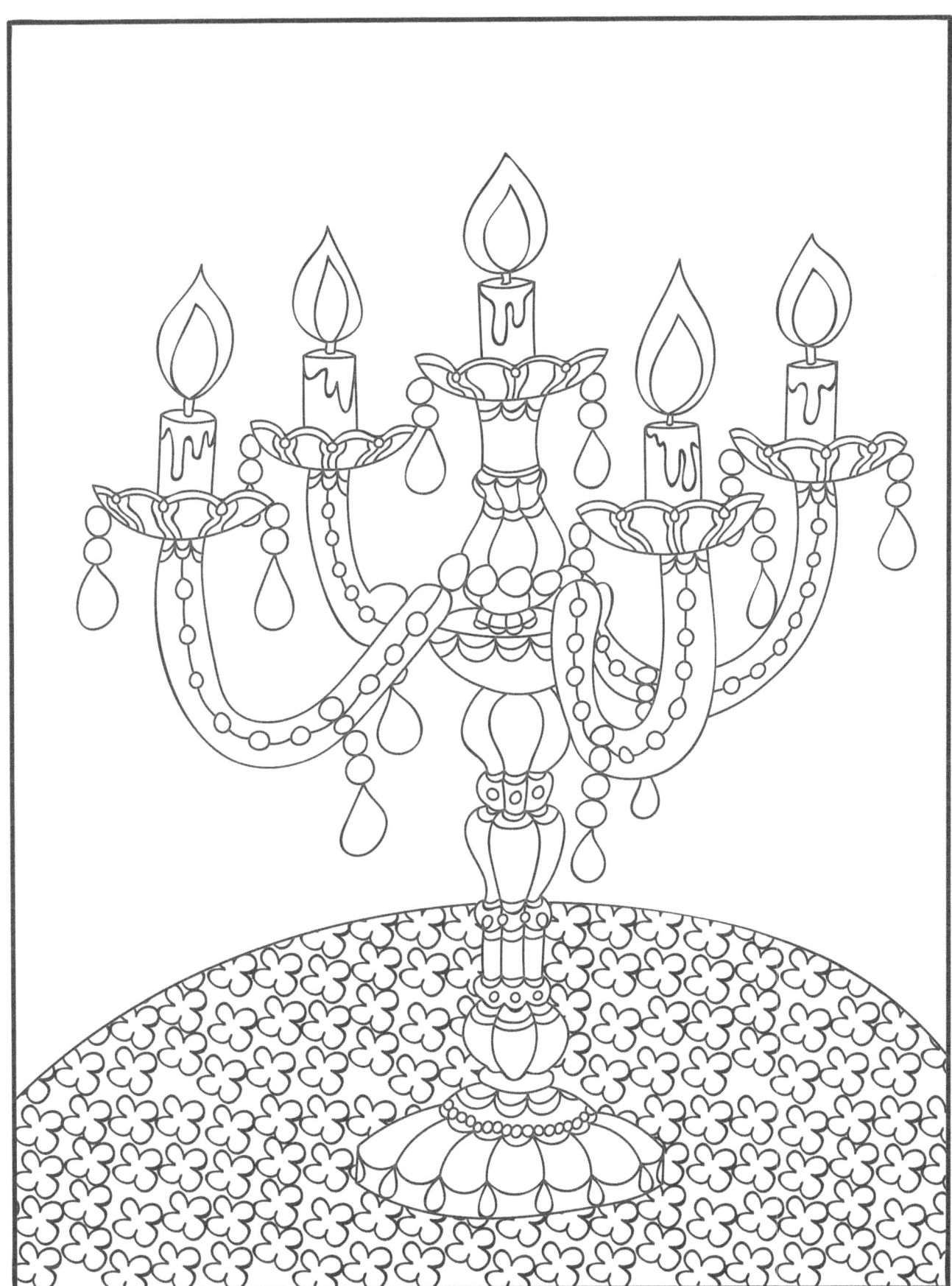

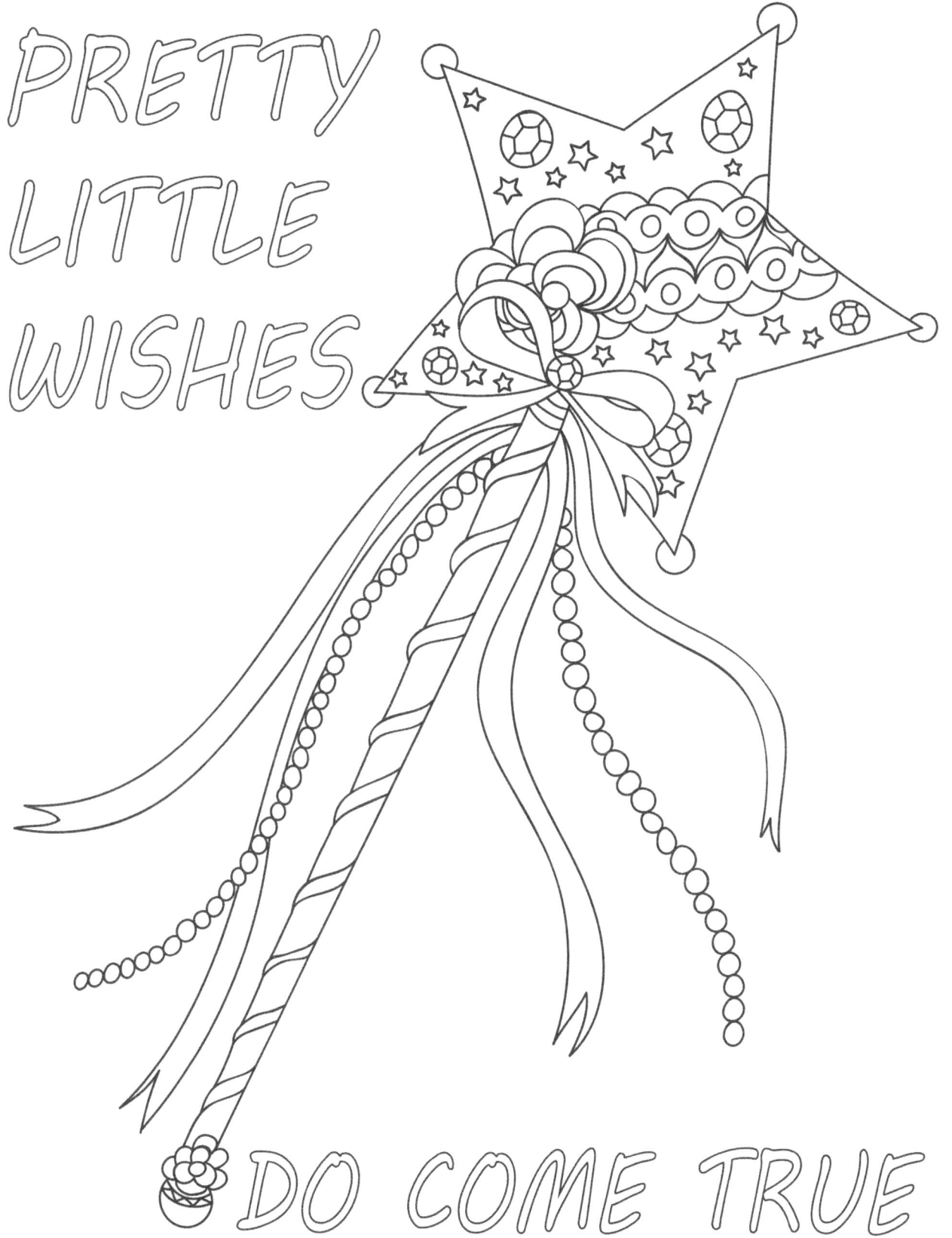

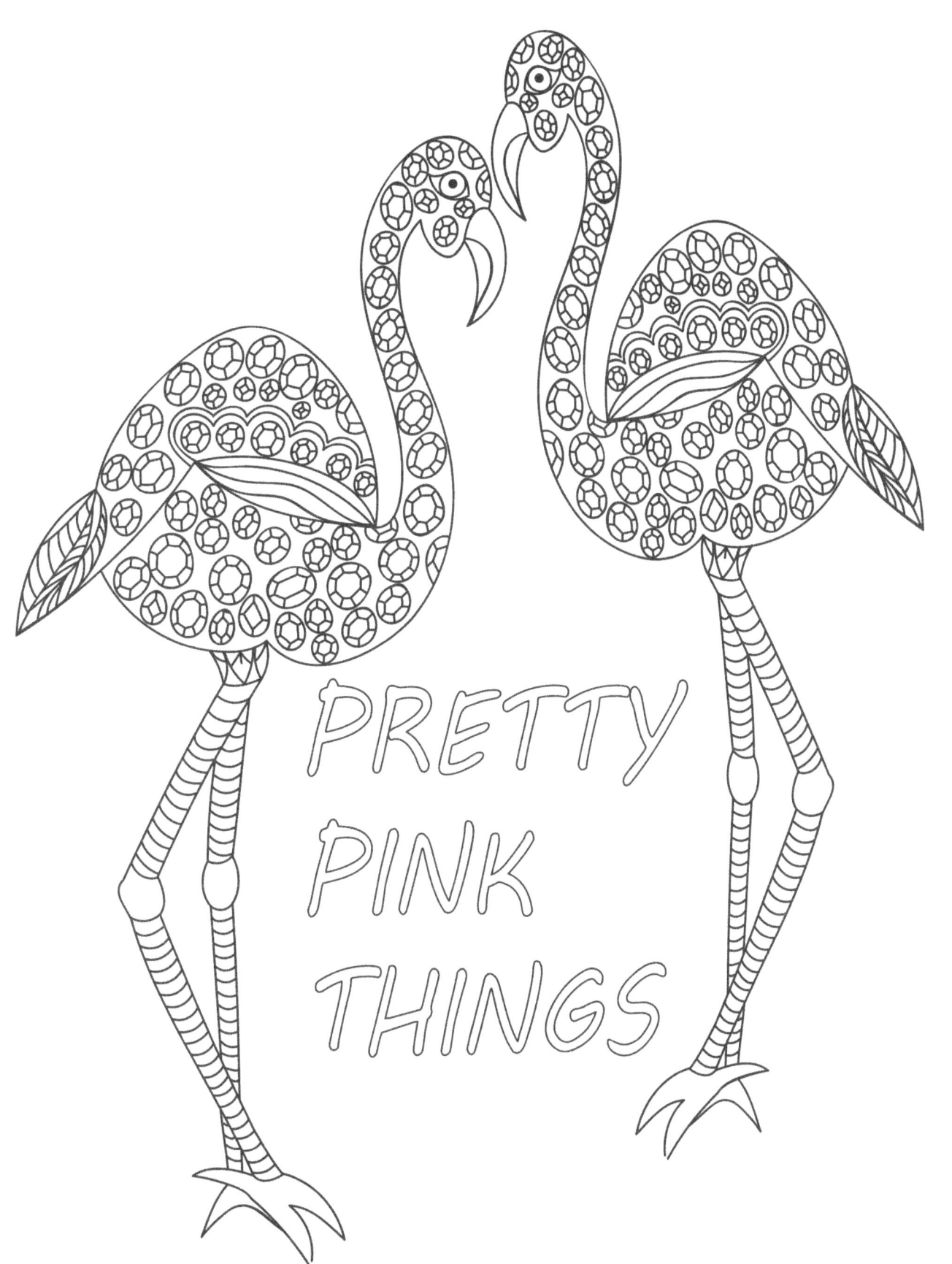

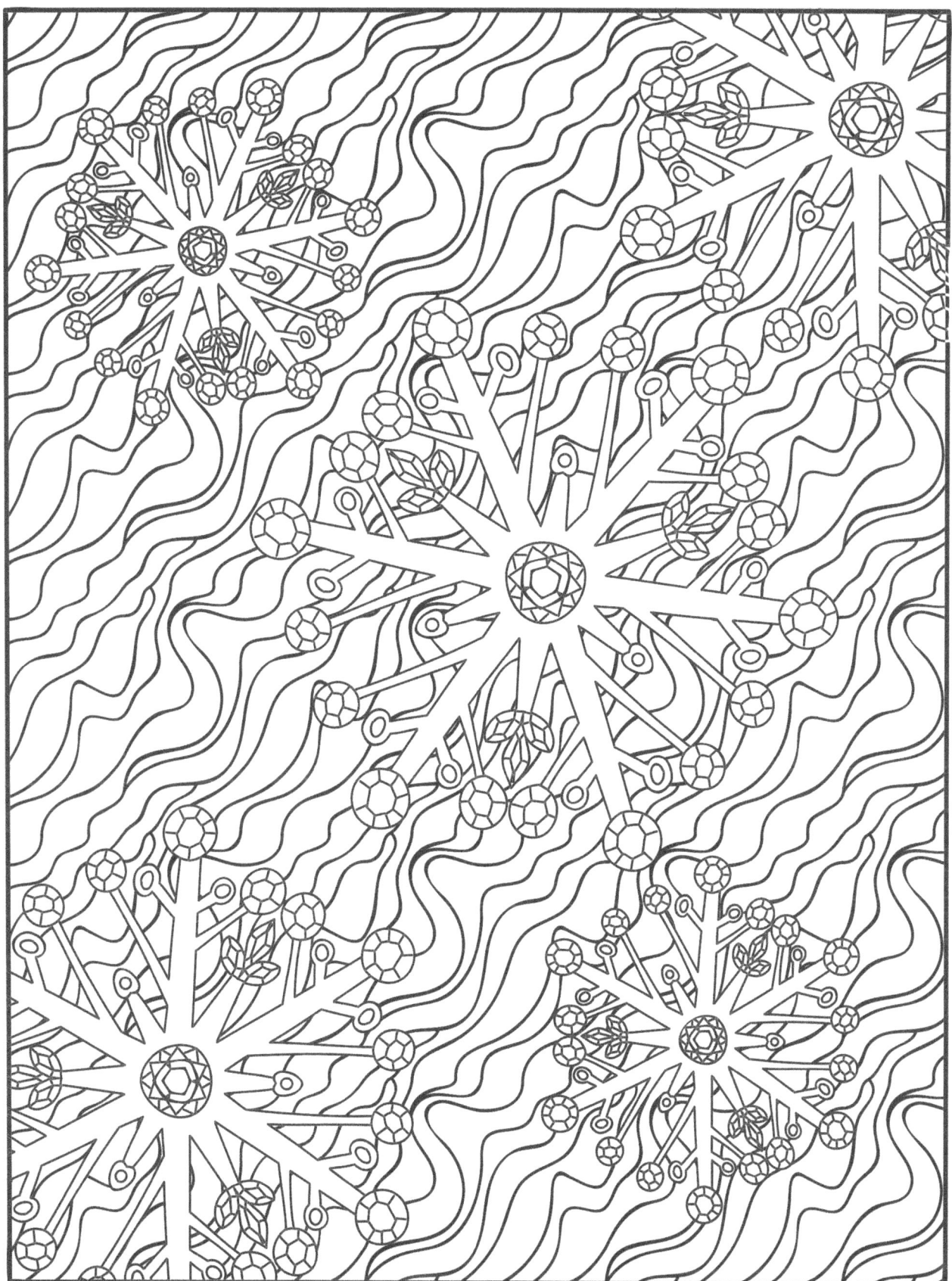

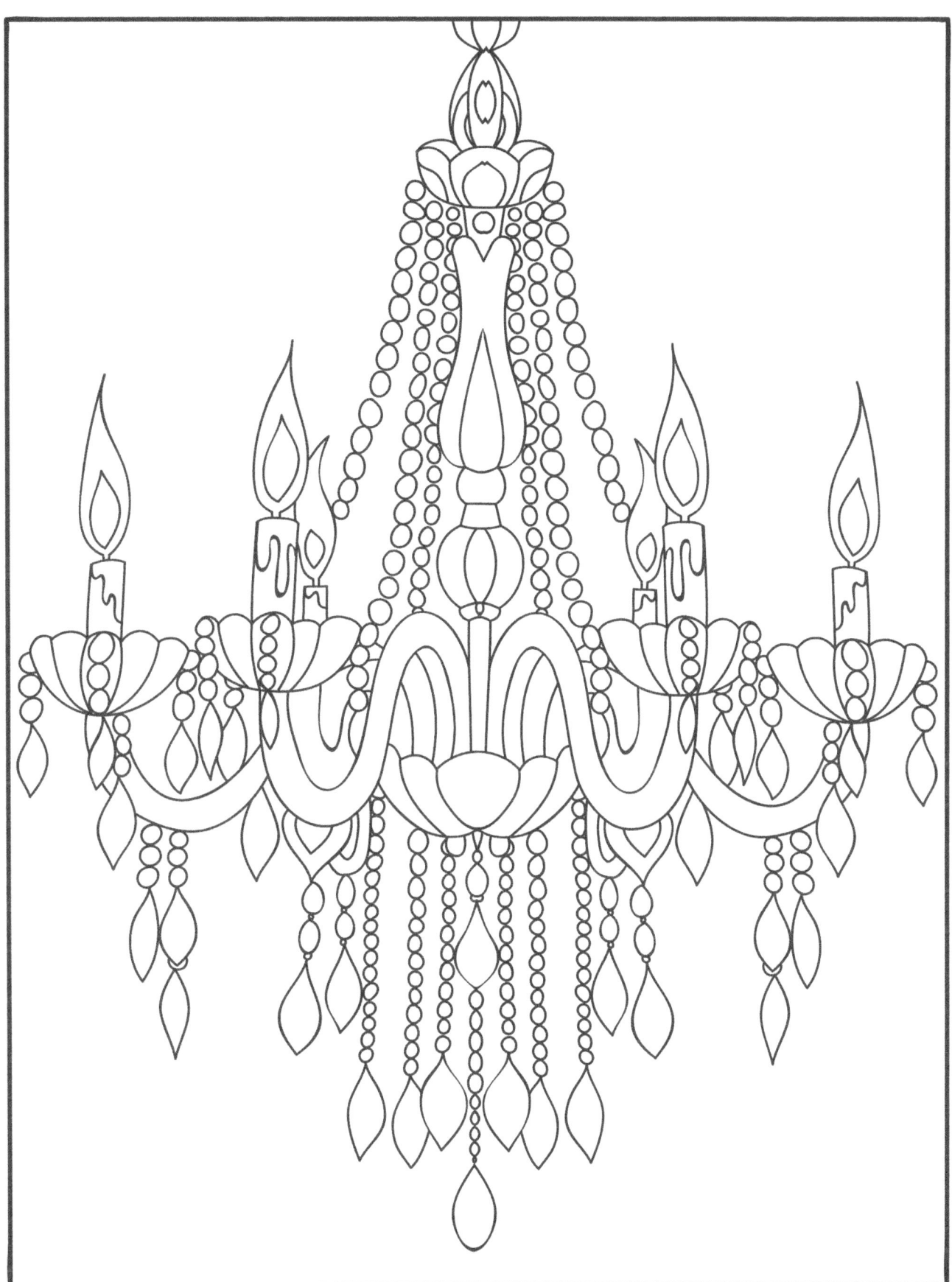

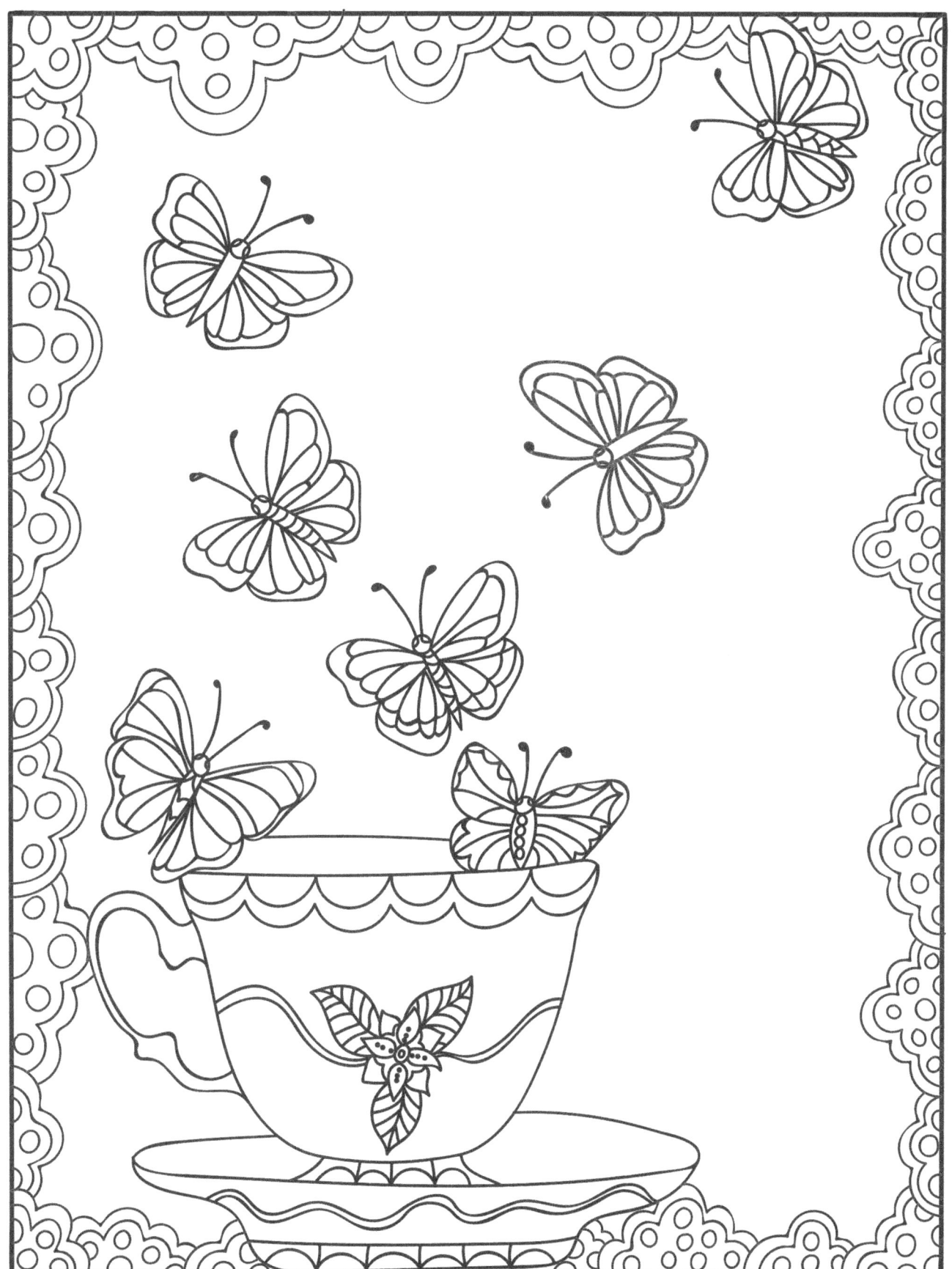

COLOR TEST PAGE

COLOR TEST PAGE

www.ingramcontent.com/pod-product-compliance
Lightning Source LLC
Chambersburg PA
CBHW081616220526
45468CB00010B/2897